# WOULD YOU RATHER

## This book belongs to:

D1532098

_____

_____

# ✶ WOULD YOU RATHER ✶

Game for two or more players.

## How to play

- The first player begins. He/she chooses and reads a question with two possible answers.
- Other players try to guess what his/her answer is.
- The first player reveals what answer he/she has chosen and the reason why.
- The winner is the player who guesses the right answer.
- Then the second player reads a question...

TIP: You can write players' points when you play in a larger group. You can play for prizes.

**have a Christmas tree cactus**

**or**

**a Christmas tree pizza?**

have Christmas

or

Easter?

✳ ✳ ✳ ✳ ✳

meet the Easter Bunny
or
Santa Claus?

**have one big cat**

**or**

**20 kittens on your Christmas tree?**

**laugh like Santa**
**or**
**talk like an elf?**

Ho, Ho, Ho,

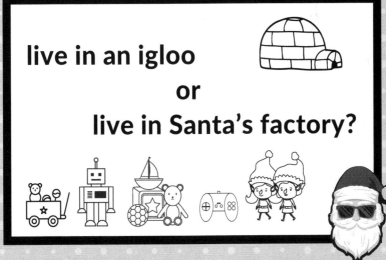

**live in an igloo**
**or**
**live in Santa's factory?**

**meet a living snowman**

**or**

**a Yeti?**

**give up one
family holiday
tradition**

**or**

**start a new one?**

**give up
Christmas trees**

**or**

**Christmas
cookies?**

get
Christmas
kisses from
a penguin

or
from a
white bear?

# WOULD YOU RATHER

be a mouse or be an owl?

be a fish or be a seal?

CHRISTMAS QUESTIONS

listen to drummers all night
or
Christmas carol singers all
week?

see Santa's
naughty
or Santa's
nice
list?

✳ ✳ ✳ ✳ ✳

receive socks

or

receive a
dictionary for
Christmas?

live with Santa in his
workshop
or
live in a gingerbread
house?

## grow a beard like Santa
## or grow
## antlers like a reindeer?

## wear a Santa hat
## or
## have elf ears?

have a carrot for a nose
like Frosty the Snowman
or
a red nose like Rudolph the
Red-Nosed Reindeer?

# WOULD YOU RATHER

**be cold as a snowman**

**or**

**be hot as the sun?**

**drive your new car
or
go sledding with
Santa all night?**

## CHRISTMAS QUESTIONS

know what all your gifts are
before you open them
or
be surprised by all your
gifts?

**put-up Christmas decorations**
**or**
**help with the cooking?**

✳ ✳ ✳ ✳ ✳

**be Santa and get stuck in a chimney**
**or be yourself but have to wear a different Christmas sweater every day of the year?**

show up to school
wearing a Santa
Claus outfit
or
a Grinch outfit?

give one gift to someone
who doesn't have any gifts
or
keep 10 gifts for yourself?

see Santa coming down the
chimney
or
have more presents than
you have ever had?

only be able to celebrate
your birthday
or
only be able to celebrate
Christmas?

**Would You Rather say "Merry Christmas" in all languages or memorize all of the Christmas carols?**

**find out Santa Claus was real or Tooth Fairies were real?**

only be able to decorate
your house with ugly
holiday decorations
or
never have holiday
decorations again?

**go sledding
or
watch Christmas movies?**

✳ ✳ ✳ ✳ ✳

**work in Santa's workshop
or
ride with him in the sled,
delivering gifts?**

## Make snow angels
## or
## go ice skating?

have really bad Christmas
presents
or
none at all?

have to write down all of the
gifts that children wanted
or
wrap all of the gifts if you
were one of Santa's elves?

## Have a hot Christmas
## or
## a snowy Christmas?

celebrate Christmas in a
snowy mountain town
or
in a sunny beach town?

be given a Christmas gift
that is fun to play with
or
that serves a purpose?

have jelly beans for eyes
or
candy cane for legs?

know exactly what presents you're getting one month before Christmas or have to wait one week after Christmas to open up all of your gifts?

✳ ✳ ✳ ✳ ✳

have to shovel snow every day during Christmas break

or

not have any snow at all?

# Have skis for feet
## or
## mittens for hands all day?

play a character in
the "Grinch"
or
"The Search For
Santa Paws"?

✳   ✳   ✳   ✳   ✳

open one $5 present
every day
or
one big present that
costs $150
once a month?

## Shovel snow
## or
## rake leaves?

## clean up all your house or clean up reindeer poo?

## have a longer Christmas break or a longer summer break?

be the only person in the entire world who didn't get a Christmas present
or
the only person who got a present?

## get one big Christmas gift
## or
## many small ones?

## talk like you're singing
## a Christmas melody
## or
## sing like you're talking?

have Christmas lights for
hair
or
a light-up nose like
Rudolph?

## stay home
## or
## go out on New Year's Eve?

## spend Christmas with family
## or
## go and visit Santa in the Artic alone?

eat only one food for
Christmas you liked
or
many dishes you don't like?

sleep through all of
Christmas Day
or
not get any good presents
on Christmas?

✳ ✳ ✳ ✳ ✳

take a ride on the Polar
Express
or
the Grinch's sled?

# meet Santa
## or
# a famous actor?

wear Santa's hat all year
or
Santa's shorts all year?

be the Grinch who stole
Christmas
or
the Scrooge who didn't
give any presents?

## meet Santa
## or
## his wife?

work as Santa at the Mall
on the weekend
or
wear a snowman costume
all week?

become Santa for one night
or
become one of his reindeers?

# watch Christmas movies all night
## or
# sing carols for money all day?

## have teeth white as snow
## or
## marry Snow White?

✳ ✳ ✳ ✳ ✳

## Decorate 10 houses
## or
## Cook 10 Christmas meals?

## talk to reindreers
## or
## elves?

Wrap 10 presents for your
friends
or
wrap your dream present
for yourself?

wear Christmas stockings
for 1 week
or
wear Christmas sweaters
for 2 weeks?

# shovel snow for 2 hours
## or
# perform in a Christmas show wearing a stupid costume?

look for the perfect gift
for ten hours
or
untangle Christmas lights
for 6 hours?

have Christmas with a
cold drink on a beach
or
Christmas in a cold place
with hot chocolate?

have the most beautiful
Christmas tree
or
the most beautiful
Christmas clothes?

eat an awful turkey
or
an awful pudding?

have Santa's belly
for one week
or
laugh like Santa for
a month?

## be hit with a snowball in your eye
## or
## fall into cold water?

wear smelly socks for
Christmas
or
smelly underwear?

read your friends' minds
or
read Santa's presents list?

**listen to Christmas music
on repeat all day
or
watch one Christmas movie
on repeat all Christmas
time?**

be as smart as Kevin in
Home Alone
or
as rich as Scrooge?

listen to Jingle Bells
all day
or
All I Want For
Christmas Is You?

**get one thousand dollars or one thousand Christmas cards?**

have your tongue frozen
or
your lips frozen?

* * * * *

get a surprise present
or
have a surprise guest at
the Christmas party?

be a wizard
or a superhero?

have lots of good friends
or a few great friends?

visit your favorite actor's
house or your crush's house
invisibly?

have an extra eye
or an extra ear?

cook or clean the house?

wash the dirty laundry
or fold up the clothes?

 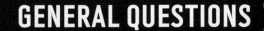

read minds or be invisible?

be bitten by a spider
or stung by a bee?

be the Tooth Fairy
or the Easter Bunny?

live in a forest
or on the beach?

have lots of superpowers for
a month or one superpower
for a whole year?

give up burgers
or ice cream?

have to wear a clown nose or a clown wig everywhere you go?

cure cancer or make sure everyone always had enough food?

live forever or be given unlimited money?

have to face a lion or a bear?

be friends with Dracula or a werewolf?

find Atlantis or El Dorado?

never have to stand in line again or never have to sit in a waiting room again?

possess the ability to know what your classmates are thinking or be completely invisible?

live in an amusement park or a museum?

fall asleep in the class or fall asleep in the cinema?

join the Avengers or the X-Men?

drink water that has soap within it or drink water that has mud within it?

always have summer or always have winter?

have the ability to time travel or to stop time?

be a human or a robot?

have to use leaves for your toilet paper or mayonnaise for your soap?

have a kitten or a puppy?

create Mickey Mouse of SpongeBob SquarePants?

eat soup with your hands or rice with a toothpick?

be friends with Superman or Spiderman?

have robots or space aliens invade our planet and take over the world?

be able to talk to pets or be able to understand all the languages in the world?

eat dog food or cat food?

have a pet dinosaur
or a robot?

kiss a jellyfish
or step on a crab?

be able to change colors like
a chameleon
or be as strong as a tiger?

be able to talk to animals
or read people's minds?

jump like a kangaroo
or be slow like a sloth?

grow whiskers like a cat,
or have to meow at the end
of every sentence?

turn into a dog or a cat for
the rest of your life?

be rich or smart?

find something you lost
or get something brand new?

be a unicorn or be a pony?

sleep in a noisy room
or in a dirty room?

have to wear a beard like Santa for your entire life or have the longest hair in the world?

have two heads or a tail?

eat a whole jar of Nutella or drink ten soda cans?

get no presents for your birthday or get presents that you don't like?

be able to see through walls or be able to hear through walls?

 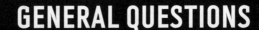

live with penguins or lemurs?

have the power to time travel or teleport to another planet?

go to a beach or to mountains?

live forever or live for 100 years?

step on a dog poop while wearing shoes but not wash it off all day or stand on dog poop in bare feet but wash it off immediately?

put your hand in a can
of worms
or a can of cockroaches?

win in a pie eating contest
or in a drinking contest?

meet your favorite singer
or your favorite actor?

always wear clothes you hate
but everyone else loves
or always wear clothes you
love but everyone else hates?

swim in a pool of mud
or slime?

eat rotten eggs
or the soles of your shoes?

let someone spit in your
eyeball
or spit in your mouth?

be a ninja or a spy?

be the Little Mermaid
or Sleeping Beauty?

celebrate your birthday
every day or once a year?

be Loki or Thanos?

only be able to wear your swimsuit for the rest of your life or only be able to wear pants and a winter coat?

get to meet your favorite band in person
or get multiple free concert tickets?

own a sports car or a yacht?

have long hair that is damaged or short healthy hair?

 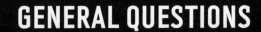

have a personal interview with your favorite actors or be in a movie with them?

have a pie thrown at your face or slime dumped on your head?

never have any homework or be paid $10 per hour for doing your homework?

eat candy whenever you want or skip school whenever you want?

have a red nose or red eyes?

live the rest of your life
with no phone
or no tv?

win an Olympic gold
medal or a Nobel prize?

live in the country
or in the city?

be in a movie
or be on YouTube?

eat something with dirt on
it or something clean but
tastes bad?

 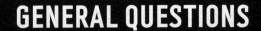

have your own pool
or live by the sea?

eat the family pet
or not eat for a week?

moo like a cow after every
sentence
or hop like a rabbit?

dress like a person from 100
years ago,
or talk like one?

have no homework
or no tests?

have one pillow or several pillows on your bed?

shower with cold water or hot water?

only see your favorite color everywhere or not see your favorite color ever again?

have a chicken's brain in a human body or have a human brain in a chicken's body?

use Nutella or peanut butter?

be an incredibly fast swimmer
or an incredibly fast runner?

become a baby again
or grow up into an adult?

break your phone
or your computer?

be good at math
or learn two foreign languages?

be a teacher at school
or the principle?

have diarrhea on a plane
that's 6 hours long
or be stuck next to someone
who does?

not be able to smell bad
smells or not be able to taste
bad food?

sleep beside a skunk or a pig?

be a famous cartoon
character or be a famous
movie star?

always be 30 minutes late
or 30 minutes early?

be constantly sneezing
or constantly have the
hiccups?

live without Netflix
or YouTube?

sleep with socks on or off?

wear an outfit of a Disney
character or a Marvel
character?

eat from a bowl like a cat
or drink from a bottle like
a hamster?

do a job you dislike and get paid well or do a job you love and make no money?

have a dead fly in the food that you ordered at a restaurant
or a hair off of the cook's body?

have the ability to understand animals or have conversations with plants?

reach Mars and live there or save the Earth and live here?

wake up with wings
or wake up with a tail?

only go to school in the summer and have the rest of the year off or go to school as we do today and only have the summer off?

have 6 fingers or 6 toes?

eat pizza each and every breakfast
or cereals and milk for every dinner?

adopt cats or dogs?

be able to sleep as late as you wish or be able to stay up as late as you like?

grow antenna like a bug or grow a bushy tail like your dog?

have to brush your teeth with a dirty toothbrush or wipe your butt with dirty toilet paper?

control water or fire?

live in a house that is too hot or too cold?

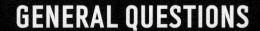

never wear shoes
or never wear underwear?

go on a two-week vacation
anywhere you want,
or get a two-month vacation
at home?

have a cat-sized elephant
or an elephant-sized cat as a
pet?

be in your favorite video
game or be in your favorite
cartoon?

eat rotten eggs
or expired milk?

become a hero
or a supervillain?

be able to change your eye
color every day
or your hair color every day?

have all snacks you need for
your entire life
or all candies you need?

be the size of an ant
or a giant?

 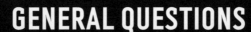

have stripes like a tiger
or rosettes like a jaguar?

have a gum stick in your hair
or step on it?

to be a shark in the sea
or a piranha in the Amazon?

spend the night alone at a
museum or camp outdoors?

be all alone in a desert
or in a jungle?

be able to see everything
or control anything?

watch any movie you like in slow motion, or only watch movies other people choose but at regular speed?

travel to the past to see living dinosaurs or travel to past to see how the pyramids were built?

your drawings come to life or your songs become reality?

never have milk to have with your cereals or never have butter to put on your bread?

speak 5 languages
or be a great writer in 1?

have one big eye in the
middle of your forehead
or have two noses on your
face?

kiss a frog or hug a snake?

be a hummingbird
or a cheetah?

be tickled by a vampire
or licked by a werewolf
every single day?

eat only vegetables
or only fruit for the rest of
your life?

brush your teeth with
mayonnaise or eat your fries
with toothpaste?

swim in a pool that has
visible poop in it
or a pool tainted with urine?

be a friend of a talking
rabbit or a magical elf?

feed an animal
or milk an animal?

ride a horse or drive a car?

cook dinner
or clean up afterward?

live without shampoo
or without toothpaste?

have a small party
every month
or one big party every year?

hold a cockroach or a worm?

be loved by every
human you see or be
loved by every dog you see?

live in a house made of doughnuts or sleep in a bed made of jelly beans?

spend all night in a bookstore or in a supermarket?

have your uncle's hair or your grandfather's mustache?

trade toothbrushes with a stranger or exchange underwear?

live in a pond with some frogs, or live in a tree with some squirrels?

**WOULD YOU RATHER**

be a friend of a magical
creature or an alien?

only eat your favorite food
for the rest of your life or
never eat it again?

have a water fight
or a food fight?

eat worms or beetles if you
had to survive?

be super strong
or super fast?

take tea or coffee?

 **GENERAL QUESTIONS**

tidy your bedroom
or classroom?

only eat sweets for the rest
of your life
or never eat them again?

be abducted by Zombies
or Aliens?

be an online influencer
or be a talk show host?

eat a dead bug
or a live worm?

ride a camel or a horse?

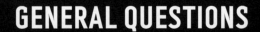

be a doctor for people
or a vet?

have a kangaroo
or koala as your pet?

have a car that could fly
or a car that you could drive
underwater?

possess the ability to smell
sounds
or be able to hear smells?

be a monkey
or a gorilla?

be a teacher or a student?

live without music
or without television?

live in a tree house
or in a cave?

be floating in a lifeboat on the
ocean or alone in a desert?

never eat chocolate again or
never kiss anyone again?

eat frozen fruit popsicles
or olives?

spoil a movie for friends that they haven't seen or have a friend spoil a movie that you haven't seen?

swim in a pool full of jelly or full of Nutella?

learn to pilot a plane
or learn to drive a race car?

own a pirate ship
or a private jet?

be able to control time
or control the weather?

see a dinosaur or a dragon?

wear your pants backward or wear your shoes on the wrong feet?

visit a lost city or a Museum?

meet a mermaid or an elf?

have a camera as your eyes or a sound recorder as your ears?

live on the Moon or live on Mars?

have purple hair or green hair?

discover a hidden treasure
or discover a living dinosaur?

have to sleep only 1 hour a
day or have to sleep 16 hours
a day?

dress up like Mickey Mouse
or Minnie Mouse?

be great at math
or great at English?

eat a bowl full of worms
or an entire frog?

be without the Internet for a week or without your phone?

sail the world or fly around the world?

live on a farm
or live in a big city?

go without television or junk food for the rest of your life?

have a magic wand
or a magic carpet?

wear your clothes inside out
or backward?

play in the rain
or in the snow?

go to the movies
or watch a movie at home?

have the ability to fly
or be able to breath under
water?

have to stay up all night
or sleep all read?